Alf Garnett has variously been described as 'a modern Falstaff', 'an Orwellian character with misplaced loyalties of Dickensian proportions', 'a kind of English fairy, an eternal type like Puck'. However that may be, Alf here reveals himself to be the uniquely ignorant, loud-mouthed, opinionated bigot who enraged and delighted twenty million television viewers, the man whose inimitable, convoluted logic defies all attempts at argument.

With the creation of Alf Garnett, Johnny Speight ('a modern Hogarth, a Swift or a Dickens') added a new figure to the familiar host of English literary characters, a figure whose name has become synonymous with all that is reactionary, bigoted, blindly prejudiced and narrow-minded. In this 'Open Letter to the People of Britain' Alf pronounces on subjects which range from Gladstone ('everyone in Wapping knew he was Jack the Ripper') to anthropology ("course, your Welsh are your first original coons') to Marx and Engels ('all their bloody shops selling Socialist rubbish'), pointing out along the way where England went wrong.

THE THOUGHTS OF
CHAIRMAN ALF

THE THOUGHTS OF CHAIRMAN ALF

ALF GARNETT'S LITTLE BLUE BOOK

or

WHERE ENGLAND WENT WRONG—
AN OPEN LETTER TO THE PEOPLE OF BRITAIN

JOHNNY SPEIGHT

Illustrated by Stanley Franklin

ROBSON BOOKS

First published in Great Britain in 1973 by ROBSON BOOKS
LIMITED 28 Poland Street, London W1V 3DB. Copyright © 1973
Johnny Speight.

ISBN 0 903895 03 X

Art Director Felix Gluck
Cover designed by David Ross

Printed in Great Britain by Redwood Press Limited Trowbridge, Wiltshire

Dedication
To H.R.H. The Princess Anne

I, Alfred Garnett, Your Royal Highness's dutiful and loyal subject, of the Borough of Wapping, London, beg leave humbly to offer Your Royal Highness my sincere and hearty congratulations on the Marriage of Your Royal Highness to Mark Phillips of Walls Pork Sausages, and thank you eternally for marrying one of us, Your most loyal subjects, and not one of your Common Market rubbish or any other foreign royal rubbish, and fervently pray that Your Royal Highness's Sacred Person an' Lovely an' Valuable Life be preserved by God for many years and may Your Mum an' Dad long reign over a free, happy and loyal people.

I have the honour to be,
With the sincerest gratitude,
And highest respect, Your Royal Highness,
Your most devoted humble servant,

Alfred Garnett, Esquire

In the Days of Yer Henry

OF course, to start with, you've got to go back to Henry the Eighth for our great days of England, when England was starting to win the world and rule it for its own good. In them days the world was run by the Pope and his Mafia, and it was Henry the Eighth who was the first to resist them and who formed the Church of England to deal direct with God and get rid of the Pope as middleman. Henry called his Bishops to him and said, 'How do we know what the Pope is telling us is the truth? I mean, the *Pope* might say it, but did *God* say it? I mean, said Henry, 'how do we know the Pope ain't telling lies, or putting words into God's mouth?' So he said, 'I don't want to know about all that Papal bull, I'll go direct to God meself as King of England and ask Him what He thinks about England Himself personally.'

'Course, the Pope didn't like this, 'cos it cut down his takings out of the plates of England. But God told Henry to ignore the Pope and to build His — God's — Kingdom on Earth here in England. And Henry said, 'So be it'. And he announced that no Mafia bride would ever sit on the throne of England, an' said that if he caught any of his wives paying dues to the Pope he would behead them. And the Mafia got banned out of the country, and went to America, with all their dons an' cardinals.

One of the first things Henry did was to buy Anne Boleyn a house right near West Ham football ground. Next door almost. And it was Henry who founded West Ham so he would have somewhere to go Saturday afternoons when he was down at Boleyn with Anne. That is why your West Ham United play in the colours of Henry the Eighth, even till this day: claret an' blue, which was his favourite drink and the blue of your Royal blood. The Directors' Box at West Ham is actually built on the spot where Henry used to sit while he watched the lads play, an' they used to bring his claret across from the Boleyn Arms.

I think it was at West Ham that he might have met Anne, 'cos she was a local girl. But she was untrue to him, and started to muck about with someone else, so he chopped her head off. He was heard to say to her down at West Ham one day, he said, 'I'm telling you, Anne. I'm giving you fair warning, if I catch you at it with anyone else, I'll give the lads your head to kick off with. I'll bung it on the centre spot next home game.' An' he did!

Yer Parliament under Henry was always sub-servant to him and his rule, and the people right throughout the whole of the country, from the West End to the East End, from Gamages to Tubby Isaacs, was loyal to the King, and he ruled in accordance with yer Magnus Carter and the popular will. He brought yer Scots to their knees at Solwyn Bay down near Hampton Park and gave the Micks a taste of English cold steel, making bloody sure they gave no more trouble during his reign. Some people said Henry ought to have educated the Micks then, but I mean, blimey, no one's ever been able to do that! I mean, that's asking too much, even of Royalty.

'Course, those were the days before them crafty Socialists Marks and Engels come over here and started all their bloody shops selling Socialist rubbish, and the labour co-ops, undercutting the British Home Stores and the Home and Colonial.

Gladstone the Jew

THE real rot started with Jack the Ripper, otherwise known as Gladstone the Jew, the scourge of the flower of British womanhood, specially in Wapping, where he lurked in the foggy streets. Everyone in Wapping knew that Gladstone was Jack the Ripper, and as people said, 'Course he's the Prime Minister, 'cos if you're going to be a sex pervert an' attack girls an' women in Wapping, what better way to remain undetected than by becoming Prime Minister?' The *last* man people would suspect. 'Cos if you happen to be the Prime Minister and you meet a copper just after leaving the scene of your foul crime, he ain't going to say, 'What're you doing here with that black bag?', is he? He's going to say, 'Hello sir, Mr. Prime Minister, Mr. Gladstone sir, how are you?' And that's how he got away with his foul perverted crimes.

But it wasn't only the people of Wapping who knew who Gladstone really was. Disraeli knew also, and so did Queen Victoria. That's why Queen Victoria wouldn't leave the safety of Windsor Castle while Gladstone was Prime Minister. She told Disraeli, she said, 'I'm not venturing out on the streets of London while Gladstone the Jew is roaming about with his little black bag'. Going round Wapping with surgical instruments attacking women and girls down there, she said, no woman was safe on the streets of London. 'Restrain Gladstone', she said, 'First put him under lock and key'.

So Disraeli brought it up in the Houses of Parliament, but he was ruled out of order by Hans Ard the German, who was the referee for all the Parliaments in them days. Hans Ard the German said it was *sub Judas* to mention Gladstone in the House in connection with

these dastardly attacks on the unprotected womenfolk of Wapping.

So, with a mass murderer as Prime Minister and the Royal Family growing weaker, England had to struggle on, and with the customers of Marks and Engels growing greater in number, a black cloud loomed over the coast of Merrie England, this once glorious land of Henry the Eighth and West Ham United.

Rule From the Top

YOU see, the country's got to be run from the top down, from Buck House, the way it was run in Henry's day. Another thing, it's an insult putting Charles in the Navy as only a First Lieutenant. He should be an Admiral. Soon as that boy said to his Mum, 'Mum, I want to be a sailor,' she should've said, 'Right. So be it. Son, the Navy's yours,' and put him in charge of it, as Admiral until he's King. An' if Andrew wants to play soldiers, give him

the Army to play with, make him a General.
Teach him how to be a real soldier. And go at it
the same as with your fox hunting—blood 'em
early. Take our young Royals to the trouble
spots—Ireland, for instance, and have the blood
of our enemies smeared on 'em. Let 'em get the
scent of war so that when they're older they can
ride at the head of their troops like Henry did,
calling 'Charlie for old England!' And, 'Blood,
boys!'

25

Yer Queen should have a veto to allow her to overrule Parliament anytime she wants to. 'Cos she's born to rule. Not like yer Labour rubbish — I mean, half of them are dragged up out of yer bloody slums. They don't even know how to wipe their noses properly, most of 'em. In the old days, when yer Kings an' Queens ran the country, we was a force to be feared. Blimey, when the first Elizabeth was on the throne the whole world shivered in their shoes, mate. 'Cos if anyone in the world gave her any old back-chat, she sent old Drake out with his fleet — a rattle of drums, mate, and he was under full sail — an' he brought their heads back for her.

Up the Hammers

I mean, one day when Elizabeth was down at
Tilbury with Drake an' his lads, and with the
Armada coming up the channel, she said, 'My
loving people', she said, 'All you here of dockland
—supporters of my father's team, West Ham.
They have told us', she said, 'to be careful of our
safety . . . to take heed how we commit ourselves
to armed multitudes, for fear of treachery from
you, my people, my loyal subjects who have
followed my father's team—West Ham—to

victories in ten cup finals'. (*That was before the Football League, when football was football, and your defence wore armour and carried bloody swords an' no bloody foreign team dared to meet us.*) 'But I assure you', she went on, 'I do not desire to live to distrust my faithful, loving people. Let tyrants fear . . . I am come among you, as you see, at this time, not for my recreation and disport . . .' (*it's true — West Ham were playing away that week*) 'but being resolved, in the midst of the heat of battle, to live and die amongst you all. I know that I have the body of a weak woman'. (*You see, there was no woman's lib about her, mate, and she was the Queen of England.*) 'But I have the heart and stomach of a King . . . and a King of England, too. And I think foul scorn that any Prince of Europe or Spain should dare to invade the borders of my realm. Rather than any dishonour should grow by me, I will myself take up arms, I myself will be your general, judge and rewarder of every one of your virtues in the field. Up the Hammers! And death to the Spanish King and his bloody Armada!'

Could you imagine darling bloody Harold doing that, eh? He'd run a mile. Look at him with Gibraltar. He should have stuffed Franco's paella down his dago throat! And I mean, just after that speech, she was having her dinner,

Elizabeth was, when Essex came in and told her they was raising armed rebellion in the city streets, and she didn't even bat an eyelid. She finished her dinner, and then took a bloody great carving knife and a rolling pin and went out on the street and said, 'Where is the rebel who will dare to face me?' And she was sixty-seven then. And the rebels, they might well have quailed, 'cos she could be a bloody rough handful when she liked. She had a piercing eye and could see through any of 'em who was after something for nothing. And when the bloody scouse gits and geordies rebelled she ordered hangings on every village green and market-place where the rebels had assembled. And the bodies, she said, was to remain there and rot till they fell to pieces where they hung. And when she was in a rage, mate, with all the rubbish around her, she left no doubt whose daughter she was, and laid about her with a big old rusty sword she kept handy. (The rust was caused by the damp of the blood that Henry her father had drawn with it.) But when she smiled — perhaps at the glad tidings that West Ham had won again — it was pure sunshine.

And her sister, Henry's other daughter, bloody Mary, was just the same. She put a few down, but only unbelievers, to save their souls. They was the good times of England, they was.

Edward's Dad

AN' look at King George before the First World War. Look what he did. He tried to avert that war, he did, God rest his soul. He invited the Kaiser, who was his cousin, over to Buck House for dinner with him. And after they'd had their dinner, King George took off his white gloves and he said to the Kaiser, 'Bill', he said, 'I don't want a war, with my men fighting your men. If we got any differences', he said, 'come out the back, an' fight it out man to man —

bare fists'. An' with that he sparred up to him. But the bloody Kaiser was scared stiff, 'cos he knew, mate, that old King George would have knocked his bloody German head off. So he wouldn't fight him. So we had to have a war. And as you know, they got their bleeding heads knocked off anyway.

Yer see, yer German's not a bad soldier. He's all right. Better'n most of yer foreigners. Well, the best of yer Germans is like us. But one thing they can't stand is the sight of cold steel. Show 'em a British bayonet an' they're off. An' old King George knew that, too. That's why he said to Kitchener, 'Fred', he said, 'issue my lads with bayonets and the Hun won't last long'. And he told his people, 'If you're in a restaurant and you find yourself being served by a foreign waiter of German descent, stand up and throw your hot soup in his face and demand to be served by someone British'.

The Traitor Baldwin

OF course, the Queen got the throne because her father was the Prince of Wales' brother. I mean, her father hadn't been trained for the throne at all, nor had her mother. I mean, her Mum, a very nice woman — a bit common as Royalty goes, but nice — well, I mean, after all, she wasn't cut out for the job. She was only a little Scottish housewife really, and never dreamt she'd ever sit on England's mighty throne. She wasn't Royalty, you see. Not *proper* Royalty. Just

Royal by marriage, that's all. So the Queen, Elizabeth the Second, to be truthful, is only half Royal — sort of half-caste Royalty. 'Cos all the Royal blood was on her father's side. On her mother's side the blood was racing blood. Book-maker's blood. An' that's where your Queen gets her horsey streak. They were a bit worried in the Palace at one time in case the children turned out jockey-size. But they ain't, thank God. Anne rides a bit, but all the boys are normal size. They ain't king-size like Henry was, but their feet touch the ground when they sit on the throne which is a blessing.

Of course, that's one of the tragedies of England — poor old Edward. I mean, you've got to pay allegiance to the Queen, because she is Royalty — got to face it, she *is* Royalty — or at least as near as you'll get to it now. But you see, our rightful King, the man the throne belonged to, was Edward. But he fell out with Baldwin. Baldwin the traitor. Baldwin betrayed Edward, and betrayed the country, completely. I mean, just because Edward wanted to marry an American girl. Well, she'd been divorced, but the point was that the Americans would have given a lot to have one of theirs on the throne, sharing the throne of England. There'd have been a lot of money in it for us. And Edward saw that. He saw that by marrying her, it was a way of getting money off the Yanks, and into the Bank of England. I mean, he'd have charged 'em a lot, and would probably have become the Emperor of America as well, and got the colony back for us. But of course, Baldwin, bloody fool, had to poke his nose into it. He was no brighter than Wilson, he wasn't.

I remember the old Prince of Wales, as he was then, my father knew him well. They was always out drinking together. Of course, he was a great West Ham fan, like Henry the Eighth. And he told my dad that there was always trouble with Baldwin. He came in the pub one night and put his arm round my dad, he was almost in tears, he was, old Edward, and he said to my dad, he said, 'Help me,' he said, 'they're after me up at Buck House. It's Baldwin', he said. 'I'll tell you who it is, it's Baldwin'. And when Edward didn't come down the pub for a few weeks, my father phoned the Palace. One of them equeeries got on the phone and said 'The Prince of Wales is not to be disturbed'. And my dad said, 'Look, you touch a hair of that man's head — you lay a finger on him — and I'm marching up from Wapping with five hundred dockers'. And he went up there to Buck House, but they hadn't touched him. He came out on the balcony and waved to my old father to let him know he was all right. And later on he came down to the pub and bought my dad a drink and said to him, 'Alf', he said, 'You might not see me here anymore. I've got to go. It's Baldwin', he said.

Edward Goes to See his Friend Hitler

SO Edward went to Paris, in France, like the old Kings used to do, and tried to raise an army, but you know what bloody cowards the French are. So he went to Germany and saw his friend Hitler. And Hitler promised to help. But the trouble with Hitler was, he was a bit mad. He'd been bitten in the neck by a bat at Bergesgadden, right in his jugular, that's what sent him wrong, and before they could get the doctors to him, nearly all his blood had run out, dripping down the steps of Bergesgadden, and onto the plains below. And most of this blood was good Teutonic blood, which is nearly as good as English blood. And they had to give him a transfusion, and the only doctor that was near to him was Dr. Goebbels, who wasn't a proper doctor, but a vet really. And he got the bloods mixed up an' gave Hitler the Jewish blood he kept for feeding his pet vampires, and it sent Hitler mad, and he wanted to own the world. And Edward said to him, 'You can't own the world, you can only have what England don't want'.

After the operation Hitler frothed at the mouth and screamed at Goebbels, 'You and your bloody bats', and bit him in the leg, and Goebbels limped from then on, dragging one foot behind the other. And the scar from Hitler's false teeth could be seen to the day he died. That's how the Russians knew who it was in the bunker.

The Hokey-Pokey
Ice-Cream Man

MUSSOLINI, another friend of Edward's and of Hitler, who was trying to re-build the old Roman Empire, used to visit Bergesgadden to play Monopoly with Hitler. And Edward told him that if he helped him to regain his throne he would give Mussolini the ice-cream concession for all England. Mussolini told Edward he would help him but that he would have to wait for a while because most of

his army was still working as waiters in Italian restaurants in London.

Where England went wrong, see—an' Churchill was duped as well—they didn't realize that what Hitler and young Musso was going to do, was attack Stalin. The Prince of Wales knew—he was Hitler's friend. But Baldwin confused Churchill. What they should have down was *join in* the attack on Stalin, an' then you wouldn't have this Russian problem now, or your Chinese problem.

Admit it, I mean, all right, so people say that Hitler killed a lot of people — millions of people — all right, so the man had his faults — give you that, no one's blameless, agree with that, but he had the right idea.

On the Shop Floor

IT'S too liberal, England, that's the trouble, far too liberal. People should take a leaf out of the football — out of the FA. I mean, if yer workers belong to a factory, they *belong* to that factory, they should be forbidden to leave it until the chairman of the factory wants to sell 'em to another factory, perhaps for a price, what they're worth, like. Most of 'em ain't worth five bob anyway. But I mean, they should stay there until the owner wants to sell 'em, till he puts 'em on the transfer list. Same as yer football — it's for their own good. Not that football's perfect. I mean, there's too much argument on the football pitch. Same as in yer industry. The referee should come on with a cane so that if a player argues he can whack their legs.

The Royal Freeze

THEY don't appreciate the Royalty in this country at all. When the Queen put in for a rise, same as yer dockers, they turned it down. She didn't go on strike, she went by the Industrial Relations Court, but they turned it down. I dunno why she let 'em. I mean, let's face it, she's got 'em over a barrel, ain't she? It's yer law of supply an' demand, annit? 'Cos she's the only person in the world who can do the job, ain't she? I mean, she's laughing, she is, yer Queen. I mean, if she turned it in — if she emigrated like, they'd all be after her. Yer only real Queen in the world, she is. Yer only real Royalty that's left, she is. I mean, yer Charles is Royalty too, but if his Mum went, young Charlie'd go with her, wouldn't he? I mean, stands to reason, dunnit? He wouldn't blackleg. He wouldn't blackleg, an' duck past no pickets to get on yer throne. Not that lad. Too loyal to his Mum, he is. No. I tell you what, yer bloody Americans wouldn't half like to have her. Eh? What? Blimey, if she went out there to that America, she'd be in that bloody White House in no time. There'd be no bloody Watergate affairs then, would there?

I mean, she'd *prefer* to stay in Buck House — well, it's more Royal, annit? I mean, better appointed all round. Got continual flush toilets up there, she has. The only continual flush toilets in the world, they are . . . I know. I know the bloke what put 'em in. He lives round the corner from us in Wapping. Even during a water shortage, he said, they have a continual flow. Oh yer, she don't have to pull no chains or nothing — no Royal ball-cocks to go wrong. Anyway, I mean, Buck House'd be nothing without her. I know bloody Wilson's after it if he ever gets in again. Always had his eye on Buck House, he has. But,

blimey, look at the mess he made of Downing Street when he was in there — left it like a pigsty, he did. Heath had to have it all re-papered before he could move in, with Wilson's bloody kids an' their jammy finger-marks all over the walls.

No, look, what I'm saying is, when that lot up there got stroppy about her rise, she ought to have threatened to pack her bags an' go. Blimey, it wouldn't have been a brain drain — it'd have been a bloody *Royal* drain — an' serve 'em right. The British government should realize that she could get bigger money out there. She could live in Hollywood. She'd get a lot of TV time, out in America. They'd give her her own show, regular, at least once a week — The Queen's Hour. And she'd come on there and talk about her little problems, an' about her dogs and what to feed your dog on. Blimey, she could do advertisements — I mean, you get adverts on there about Chunkymeats an' all that, but the Queen could come on and say, I feed my corgis on whatever meat she feeds 'em on, and then you'd know that your dog could eat Royal food, just like a Royal dog. And she could give a few racing tips. I mean, she's got one of the finest racing stables in Europe, she must know when one's going to win. She could let the punters know.

I mean, blimey, yer Yanks would have paid *millions* to have her out there making 'em all Lords an' Sirs. Eh? There'd have been yer Lord Nixon right away. An' that Agnes Spiro — blimey, she'd rather go out with the Queen than Frank Sinatra, she would. And I tell you what, yer Labour lot would be the first to try an' buy her back, 'cos without her, where are they going to get all their bloody titles from, eh?

An' Philip, I mean, he should have a rise too, he should get a pay increase. 'Cos I mean, it stands to reason, dunnit, he can't afford to live up to her standards without a bit of money in his pocket, can he? I mean, the man's got his pride, an he? An' he's got to be able to call his shout, an he? I mean, he don't want people going round whispering about him not pushing the boat out, does he?

Punter Harold

I mean, an' there's yer politicians sitting up
there in that Parliament copping their twenty
thousand a year an' doing nothing for nobody.
Of course, I know they won't admit to getting
their twenty thousand. But what they tell us
they get an' what they bung in their pockets is
two different things, annit? Perks. That's what
it is, mate. Perks. *Bloody perks.* You can't tell me
that Labour rubbish can afford to live up there
the way they do on what they're supposed to be

earning. Gerroorf! They ain't got nothing of their own. They ain't got a pot to piss in, none of 'em. They ain't got no private fortunes, not like yer Tories. I mean, it's because yer Tories have got money they don't *need* to fiddle. They can afford to be honest.

I mean, look at old Wilson—bloody darling Harold. I mean, one election when he was Prime Minister he won thousands off William Hills. I

mean, see, it's a known fact what he done. See, everyone was betting not only who'd win the election, *but when it would be.* And the only man in the country who knew when it would be was Wilson—darling bloody Harold. Because it was him who had to choose when it would be. So before he announced the date, he had all his runners out round the betting shops putting his money on. And he didn't let no one else in on it—not him—not crafty Harold. No. 'Cos if he'd told the rest of his party what he was going to do, it'd have spoilt his odds, with all the rest bunging on bets.

No. He nipped round through the back door of Buck House an' told the Queen, 'I'm going to absolve the Parliament, Your Majesty.' And before she'd had time to put her crown on even, he'd shot off to collect his winnings. And he didn't even have the grace to put a bet on for her or Philip.

It was the same when he was dishing out all the country's money to the bleeding unemployed. Fifteen and sixteen quid a week for layabouts to stay at home. It's all right him dishing out money to bloody layabouts—but what about us? *Us* who has to pay for it? *Us* bloody fools what are still working? That's why they all voted

Labour, that lot. Hoping to get put out of work, they was. Banking on it, most of 'em. Well, it's your Socialist manifesto, annit? Take all the money off the rich an' give it to the poor. Put all the poor out of work to lead a life of leisure, an' let the rich keep 'em. Vote catching, that's all it is.

Tory an' Proud of It!

ALL right. So I'm a Tory. Tory an' proud of it. I got nothing against the working classes, but what I say is, they should keep to their proper function. An' their proper function ain't sitting up there in that Downing Street upsetting the laws of nature. I mean, look, you have an army, but you don't run the army with working-class Generals, do you? Look at yer church. You show me a bleeding working-class Bishop. Eh? *Show me a Bishop what lives in* *a council house.* Or a Pope what goes to work on a bike. It makes yer sick, it do, what they've done to this country — *Labour.* What we should do really, before it's too late, is move out to Australia and take the Royal Family with us.

Look at that senile old Attlee. Look at what he gave away to yer wogs. Look at a map. Just look at it. An' see where all them bloody great red bits have gone. Blimey, the countries we give away! I mean, all that lot we gave away, an' only kept this little bit. What we should have done is kept all the rest, an' give this little red bit here away — *England.* I mean, that's your bloody Labourites for you. They not only gave it all away, they gave the best bits away. I mean, there's all yer bloody wogs sitting out there in the sun surrounded by bloody oil wells, an' there's all us over here in the bleeding rain an' fog an' snow, catching colds an' bronchitis. *We've never had it so bloody bad, we ain't.*

The Original Reds

I mean, when we was out getting our Empire, we went for all the big countries. All those countries that were owned by us and ruled by us in the days of our Empire were painted red on the map — great big splurges of red. I mean, we started the movement of painting the world red. That's where the Communists got the idea from, of going red. That is why, when yer Russians started to steal countries and enslave them under the yoke of Russian imperialism, they painted the countries they stole red, just to entice immigrants into them, knowing full well that any person in his right mind would not wish to emigrate to anywhere but England — England, the land of the free, ruled by people of noble birth and not by any jumped-up Tom, Dick or Harry out of your Labour Party.

That's where yer Tories go wrong, see, with that colour blue. I mean, they were the original reds — *the original reds.* Everything they grabbed they painted red. I mean, it's in the flag — there's more red in the flag than there is blue. The blue in the Union Jack should be taken out of it, and the Tory Party should claim its rightful colour — red.

I mean, you can always tell a pure white man when he goes out in the sun — he turns red. 'Course, you get some people who look white on the surface, but you put 'em out in the sun — that's the test — and they go brown: the tarbrush comes out in 'em immediately. But a pure white man goes red first of all. You see 'em in all the seaside resorts — you can pick out the English ones — *they're red.*

That Grammar School Twit

LOOK at Heath — calls himself a sailor! I mean, blimey, that Drake in his day used to go out on his boat and bring back Spanish treasures. He looted the Spanish mainland — put it to the sword. But Heath, that bloody grammar school twit, goes out on his boat and all he brings back is Admirals Cups — not a bloody use to anyone, he ain't.

He's turned out to be another Gladstone,

betraying the flag, going into Europe with all yer foreigners. Not saying he's Jewish. But he's not proper Tory. That's why Australia's breaking away and changing the National Anthem. And who can blame them? I mean, they fought in the war, yer Anzacs did, they done more fighting than the bloody French. I mean, yer bloody Frenchies packed up after the first few weeks. Very bad at fighting, the French are, always. Never be any good as fighters. Sex and bloody food, that's all they're good for, and waiters.

And don't tell me Napoleon was French! He wasn't. He came from Corsica, which is just off yer Isle of Wight. Conquered the bloody French almost on his own, singlehanded, with one arm — well, stump, really. He lost his hand — that's why he kept it tucked in his weskit, out of sight.

I mean, Napoleon was like Nelson and Wellington. As a boy, Napoleon stared across the water at England an' it was his ambition to make good here. But he couldn't get started here as a soldier because of Nelson and Wellington, so he went to France 'cos they hadn't got any there. And he trained the waiters of France into a formidable army — well, by *their* standards anyway. 'Course, they're a bit like the Arabs,

really, yer French. Wash in the toilet, same as yer Arabs.

Before yer British went out there yer Arabs used to ride about on camels covered in flies. Now they've all got Rolls Royces. Give the Arabs their due, though — they don't get married like we do and have just the one woman. They have about forty or fifty. Even the poorer ones have one for each day of the week, and a couple on Sundays for a bit of fun, like. Then they have the Monday wife to do the washing, Tuesday's wife comes in and cleans the house out, the Wednesday wife comes in and does the shopping for the week, an' so on. The Saturday afternoon wife you can take to yer football. I mean, yer average wife you can't take to football, you don't want to be seen out with her, do yer. Then Sunday, you got your Sunday wives. That's how they work out there, and we should do the same over here in England.

The Welsh Wog

'COURSE, your Welsh are your first original coons. I mean, they all talk like Pakistanis. They were brought over here as slaves years ago from the Colonies, and put in barracks in Wales, like Amen's Asians were, in Air Force hangars and sheds — anything they could find. 'Course, being coons they weren't too particular. And they brought them to Wales 'cos Wales in them days was just one big field with coal under it. And

they put all these Welsh coons to work in the mines. But being underground so long and out of yer sun, the black wore off their skins and they turned white — well, whit*ish*. And that's why Enoch's so upset, 'cos Enoch is Welsh, and black also himself. That's why Enoch only attacks yer blacks what live in Birmingham, and never comes out in the open and attacks all yer blacks, wherever you find 'em — like yer Welsh coons who've been getting by unnoticed for years. That's why Churchill would never let Enoch take any office at all in his government — except sanitary orderly, perhaps. Because Winston knew that Enoch was a wog, the same as Disraeli knew that Gladstone was a Jew, and just masquerading as English.

Sex on the National Health

'COURSE, I blame Lord Longford for all the pornography in the country. He's not a real Lord — bloody Labour MP, he was. That's the danger of appointing Labour rubbish into the House of Lords. I mean, there was no such thing as porn in England until he imported it all from Denmark — I s'pose, originally, for the House of Lords. And if it'd been kept in the House of Lords it would've been all right, 'cos they're high-born men and know how to behave. They know how to handle your porn, they do. They only do their pornographic things with a certain type of woman, who has been bred to porn use.

The aristocracy has always had those sort of things in their household. I mean, yer Caesars had it, yer old Popes, an' all, they all had their girls for fun. They helped 'em to relax, took the worries of the world off their shoulders. I mean, same as Henry the Eighth, he didn't only have eight wives, he had all his other women too. He had his fancy bits, but then, he was Royalty. That's all right for Royalty.

It was yer Labour that started all yer free sex. Talk about Meals on Wheels—they'll want *sex* on wheels before long. They'll have the family doctor prescribing it soon, writing out prescriptions—three blondes and a brunette to be taken before meals. Let's face it. Sex ain't a thing the working class is used to. Not proper sex—having babies, yes, but not *proper* sex. I mean, you can't expect a working man to come home from a long day's work and entertain his wife with sex when he might want to watch telly or go up the pub. See, it's aping yer aristocracy.

That's where yer Lord Longford got the idea from. Aping yer Lord Lambton and yer Lord

Jellicoe. I mean, them men is used to sex. I mean, they're descended in a direct line from Henry the Eighth. They're used to having their sex with a certain type of girl that was born for that purpose. I mean, the aristocracy have always had wives which they used purely to have their heirs, someone to carry on the line after them. But, I mean, sex was treated like foxhunting—sexual sports. Something thrown in with yer roast beef and claret—all harmless. Just sport. And the girls were grateful to have been noticed. I mean, for an ordinary village girl to have been in the Royal bed—blimey, that was something to tell the children about. And the children—if they was sired by the Lord—was a cut above the rest. They became the sires of the land—squires and magistrates—*aristocratic bastards.* They was given the sort of jobs that the peasants weren't up to and the aristocracy was too busy to do.

But all this fuss with Lord Lambton and Jellicoe that yer bloody Socialist press got hold of—I mean, that was espionage. Playing yer Russians at their own game. Them whores they got was bugged. I mean, what better place to have your bug than in your whore herself? They had tape recorders sewn into their minds. You might say, how could they get a tape recorder into the mind of a woman, which is so small? And the answer is, yer Japanese. They can make a tape recorder smaller even than a woman's mind. And yer Lord Lambton and Jellicoe knew that. And what better way to bug an embassy than to have a whore in every bed — bed bugs? So that, even if they talk in their sleep their secrets leak out. They was only doing the same as yer Nixon's lot in Watergate. I mean, they were only putting whores in to bug yer Democrats.

Or, most probably, Lord Lambton and Jellicoe were just trying them out for export — just supplying certain types of girls to yer Eastern Potentates, yer Arab Oilynesses, combatting inflation and building up England's trade. 'Cos, see, when you're dealing with your Eastern Potentates, when you're after their oil, it's better to offer 'em girls now instead of camels. You go out there with your beads and bits of broken glass for 'em, and your painted hussies. All Lord Lambton was doing was getting the parcel ready. *'Course* he had pictures taken with 'em, that was just advertising. It was to show yer Arabs that these was 'girls as used by yer aristocracy', and not just any old rubbish. I mean, they don't want any old kind of woman, do they? They want to buy stuff that lives up to the standards of what yer aristocracy would use. I mean, they don't want any rubbish that Labour peers have mucked about with. Anyway, yer Labour peers can't do it, 'cos the sort of girls they fancy is titled girls, but no titled girl's going to get into bed with a Labour peer, is she? 'Cos she knows they ain't *real* aristocracy. She knows they've jumped up out of Wapping or somewhere.

Talk about a permissive society — blimey, admit it, I mean, *we* used to have a beer an' all that, you know, and get the birds drunk, like — give her a few Green Goddesses, that sort of thing, and take her down Lovers' Lane afterwards, or Cody's Road, for a little bit. But I mean, they was special sort of girls, we didn't go with the *ordinary* girl like that. I mean, we didn't tread on each other's toes, like. There was a certain type what you kept aside for marrying, but there was other sorts of special ones you had for your bit of fun, *you know*. But, blimey, these days they'd even have your daughter if you didn't watch out.

Mary Whitehouse — now that's a pure woman, but where she goes wrong, see, she don't go far enough. I mean, clean up TV by all means, but she ought not to stop there. She should clean up the whole of England — railway carriages an' all. And get all those who don't fit into her pure ways exported, all of 'em. Let 'em immigrate. Put Mary Whitehouse in charge of immigration, her an' Enoch.

Handy-Sized Coons

BEFORE the war started we was experimenting out in Australia, trying to solve the black question. What we was doing there, you see, was trying to breed 'em smaller, even smaller than the aboriginals. You see, yer aboriginals is a decent handy size for the blacks, but bred a bit smaller they could be even handier. Ideal for chimney sweeping—even have five of 'em sitting under the bonnet of your car pedalling it. An' that's what we was doing, experimenting, like they do with your dogs. You see, your big dogs breed down to little miniature dogs, an' we was trying to breed yer coloureds down to little miniature blacks. But of course, the war put a stop to all that and they went on breeding any old how, an' have grown to all sorts of awkward sizes.

Miniature blacks would have been a very handy size to have about the house. I mean, you'd only need a dog kennel or a little shed to put 'em in, and they'd have been very handy nipping about the house cleaning out the ashtrays, peeling potatoes, and all them sort of little woman's jobs. It would have put an end to this question of woman's lib too, wouldn't it? Not too late — could breed 'em fast. Put up a four-year plan to breed aboriginals for import into England — it would solve your woman's lib completely.

Women's Lib

OF course, yer woman's lib is a lot of daft talk, that is, a lot of old cobblers, 'cos yer women ain't got the same size brain as a man, have they? I mean, yer woman's brain is hardly bigger than a coon's brain. Darwin said we was descended from monkeys. Well, he was wrong. *Women* might have descended from monkeys. But *man* didn't, 'cos man is definitely a higher species. Man was made by God. And when God first created man, he created Adam all on his own in the Garden of Eden. And when God could see that man couldn't quite manage on his own, if he was going to do God's high business, he made woman as a kind of domestic, a home help, someone to fetch and mend for him, and bear him children and keep 'em clean about man's house. Blimey, the last thing God thought of was woman. Woman is a parrysite, a sort of leech, 'cos she can't live without man, whereas man can live without her.

Man: Noble, strong, intelligent.

Woman: Strawberry, raspberry, vanilla.

Woman's Place is Under Ma

THE way with women is, you've got to train 'em properly from the start, 'cos they're rather like dogs in a way. They're cleverer than dogs, I'll give 'em that. And of course, being that bit cleverer, they're more useful about the house than dogs. But as with a dog, they need a master, or owner. They're not used to thinking for themselves, or being out on their own, or doing things on their own. *A woman that's not owned by a man is always* *unhappy, and fretful.* So when you've picked out the one you want, one that takes your eye, be firm from the beginning but kind, and you will find them friendly little creatures, and easy to live with, so long as they have been trained to your needs. Always keep 'em on a short lead, exactly as you would with a dog, and don't let 'em roam.

I s'pose yer woman is a bit like yer coon in some respects. Like yer coloureds, they're all right on the buses, but they shouldn't be allowed to do anything above that. 'Course, in modern days now there is some women that used to be men. They're yer trans-sexuals. The point is, *they was never really men at all.* They was men with women's brains, and was made when God was probably a bit busy. God, you see, when he was making man, He made him like when they're making Rolls Royces, which are special. But yer women, they're made like Fords, on a conveyor belt, with a few nuts missed here and there. You can get a woman being born who looks a bit like a man but is really a woman, and after a little operation is turned back into what she should be — a woman. That is why you never get a woman turned into a man because a man, as I say, is made especial by God.

Like, I mean, take yer Queen — Elizabeth. With all due respects, she is not a man. She was made really to be the *mother* of a King, but not to rule herself. You see, if it was possible to turn a woman into a man, yer Harley Street surgeons would've turned her into a man as soon as they realized she was in line for the throne, and then of course she'd have been King Elizabeth. And they could have changed Philip's sex and made him Queen Philip. But yer Harley Street surgeons knew they couldn't make a woman into a man, like you cannot make chalk out of cheese. But you can make nearly anything into a woman, anything you like. Just put a skirt on it and it's a woman. Perhaps not everyone's idea of a woman — not the sort you'd want to marry — but good enough.

You've got to treat a woman like you would a dog. I mean, it's all in that song:

> *'She might look weary,*
> *She might look dreary,*
> *Wearing that same old shabby dress —*
> *But show a little bit of tenderness.'*

Like a dog. With care. I mean, if it looks a bit down, give it a pat on the head. Say, 'Come on, gal, 'course I loves you. I lives with you, don't

'She might look weary,
She might look dreary,

Wearing that same old shabby dress—

But show a little bit of
tenderness.'

I?' See, it takes its mind off — what mind it's got. It ain't got much, we know. I mean, take yer German Drear. Might look like a man, give you that. But she's *definitely* a woman. It's been *proved*. Anyway, you can tell that soon as it opens its mouth. I bet her father's sorry he married her mother.

You've never seen a woman amount to nothing, have yer? I mean, you get a few midwives—that's about as far as they go, helping each other bring kids into the world. But I mean, there's no women Picassos, is there? No women Harold Robbinses or Mickey Spillanes. No, they're all right for a few years when they're young, then when they're aged—useless, to man or beast.

I mean, they've had a couple in the Houses of Parliament, but only for a laugh and to issue out tea and blankets during the all-night sessions. I mean, no one's ever took them serious. What I mean is, you've never ever seen a woman Prime Minister of England. Or anywhere. *Nowhere in the world is there a woman Prime Minister.* Except in Israel—yer Goldwyn Meyer. And that's only because her husband,

being Jewish, put the country in his wife's name — an old Jewish dodge that is, to avoid tax and bankruptcy. And there's that Mrs. Nero, the Pakistani Prime Minister. But then, of course, all yer Pakistanis and Indians look like women anyway. 'Course, most of them are borderline. I mean, it's part of their religion. They even think a man's going to give birth to a baby out there — bloody fools. I mean, a man can't have a baby. I mean, his manly brain wouldn't allow him to bother with things like that — having babies.

Anyway, as I say, they're all on the borderline out there. They all wear women's dresses, masquerading as men. But you can soon tell. Put 'em up against a regiment of Guards and you'll soon see they're women. They'll gather up their skirts round their ankles and be off — wouldn't even stop to brush the flies off 'emselves. That's why yer British Intelligence dressed yer Black Watch in skirts. They put 'em in skirts, see, to try and fool the Indians that they was women too. 'Course, they soon realized when the bloody Jocks charged 'em — they gave 'em women! Blimey!

Long-haired Rubbish

BLIMEY, with our music, at least there was a bit of melody to it, least you could understand the *tune*. I mean, we had Hutch, didn't we, I mean, we had Bing Crosby and Rudy Valley, Charlie Coons and Rabbits and Landower. This long-haired stuff, there's no tune to it, is there? It's all bloody guitars all twanging. I mean, they can't play the piano, any of them. I mean, the piano was a good instrument. I mean, with a piano, even if you couldn't play it, it was nice in your front room with a few pictures on it. You can't put a bloody guitar in the front room with pictures on that, can you? They're useless bloody instruments.

I mean, George Formby and his banjo — I mean, he could play it, *he* could, ol' George. 'When I'm Cleaning Windows' and 'Chinahouse Blues' an' all that bit. Marvellous, he was, ol' George Formby, but none of them kids can play like him. They ain't got the fingers for it. They all have to have it all electrified, they do, with microphones. I mean, our singers could sing without microphones. They could belt out a song — this lot can't. Long-haired gits. They might look like Shirley Temple, but none of them can sing like 'er. I mean, blimey, if you turned off the electricity you wouldn't hear 'em. Waste of electricity most of 'em are, anyway. *Our* singers had gas only. Couldn't sing through gas — had to sing with the human voice. No aids to the human voice at all, they didn't have. Rudy Valley had a megaphone, but it wasn't electric though — didn't plug in anywhere. He still had to bellow through it, like a loudhailer.

The Windsor/Walls Alliance

WE'RE the envy of the world, we are, having a Royal Family. It's the one thing in the world no one else has got. An' don't talk to me about Norway, and Holland, and Sweden and all that rubbish. I'm talking about *Royalty*. Not bloody cloth-cap kings riding about on bikes. I mean, that's not Royalty. You'll never see our Queen on a bike. She wouldn't demean herself. Our Royalty come out in golden coaches, horses and armies behind 'em, because they're *real* Royalty, they are.

That's why you can understand Princess Anne not wanting to marry one of them. She's marrying one of us — a young lad out of the army. 'Cos she flatly refused to marry any of yer foreign rubbish. It's no good saying her Mum did, 'cos when she married him she didn't know she was going to be Queen. And again, he's not *really* foreign rubbish. I mean, all right, he's Greek and they're all foreign rubbish, admit that, but he was brought over here at an early age so he could absorb our English culture.

He lived with Lord Louis Mountbatten, who is probably more royal than the Queen. 'Course, that was the cause of the First World War, 'cos Lord Louis was the rightful Kaiser. But he was too English for the Germans and it was Hindenberg that didn't want an English Kaiser sitting on the royal throne of Germany. And Lord Louis said to Hindenberg, 'You can stuff yer bloody Germany, my sword fights for England and St. George'.

And with that he come over here, took charge of the Navy and invented the submarine. That is the kind of man who brought Prince Philip up. He saw good in the boy when he first set eyes on him, and said, 'I'm not going to let them turn him into a waiter, 'cos I know his mother' — who was a Queen of Greece.

I mean, all the Greeks is fit for is owning restaurants. 'Course, they ain't really got no royal family — never have had — never had the flair for it. I mean, yer Greek King was all right so long as he was King of Claridges, but soon as he left Claridges he looked the same as anyone else, and cab drivers didn't even stop for him. Constantine, who is the last of the line, will probably open a restaurant near Buck House, selling his moussaka and Turkish coffee to Peter Sellers and all yer film stars. Perhaps Philip will drop in from time to time for the odd meal. And p'raps, when Constantine learns to speak English proper, Charlie Forte might put him back in charge of Claridges and his motorway cafes.

But the boy Princess Anne is marrying is the son of Walls sausages, which is *good* sausages, the finest sausages made in the world. Like their ice-cream was the finest ice-cream — the 'Stop me and buy one' firm that Mussolini had set his heart on owning. Them sausages are Royally Appointed to the Queen and her father before her, and have been a delicacy of England since Henry the Eighth. In fact, Henry ate his

first Walls sausage watching West Ham play Serfs United at Boleyn in Upton Park. It is a far better delicacy than your hamburger, which the czars of Russia introduced to America after they was deposed by your communist swine Stalin and all his lot, and which Romanov still serves with that vodka he makes in his cafe in Los Angeles. Your Russian royalty is no longer there — your *real* czars, who ruled Russia before Stalin invented the commy-czars — yer *common* czars — what rule there now. Yer *common* czar of Russia is nothing like yer real czars who lived in palaces. Your *common* czar lives in a two-up, two-down slum with outside toilet like all your Labour rubbish do over here.

Now that Princess Anne is marrying into the hierarchy of the ice-cream empire and sausages, Prince Charles might also go for his bride in British industries the same way. And one of the mightiest of these is Heinzes baked beans, which Henry always enjoyed with his Walls sausages — another gift that England has given to the world. I mean, yer Princess Alexandra has already married into yer steak houses — yer Angus Steak Houses. Well, you can't blame them, can you, with your Socialists not giving them their bloody wage claims. I mean, Philip was saying the other

day that the Royal Family's hard up, so that's cleared up now with Wall's money behind them. And if the other kids marry into Woolworths or C & A, they'll be able to tell yer Labour or any government to stuff their bloody wages, and they'll rule from the City.

Rise Like Lions!

AND before they do, the people of England must rise and wave the flag, and let their Royal Majesties know that we, the people of this country, England, want a *Royal* Family in Buck House, not a family of bloody grocers!

And let us all live bravely under the flag we love, the pure white flag of England. 'Cos the flag of England *is* pure white. The red on that flag is the red of the foreign blood that was spilt in gaining our Empire. And the blue on that flag is the blue blood of yer aristocracy that spilt all the red blood. That is why even till this day, any warring countries what demand peace or talk surrender terms always wave the white flag which is the pure white flag of England, not because, as some traitors think, it's a coward's flag, but because they know that the pure white flag of England cannot be attacked by anyone without incurring the wrath of the British Lion. *White is our colour, and always has been our colour, and will always be our colour!*